Jane Prendergast.

5th, 6th
Sept. 003.

Denman

Hunter Beaumont.

GW00671449

On Life & Other Paradoxes

APHORISMS AND LITTLE STORIES
FROM BERT HELLINGER

Living Solutions
P.O. Box 616, Cork, Ireland.

Tel: INT'L Code + 353 21 4314300
Fax: INT'L Code + 353 21 4961269

e-mail: livhaz@indigo.ie
Website: www.livingsolutions.ie

On Life & Other Paradoxes

APHORISMS AND LITTLE STORIES
FROM BERT HELLINGER

Translated and with an introduction
by Ralph Metzner

Zeig, Tucker & Theisen, Inc.
Phoenix, Arizona

Library of Congress Cataloging-in-Publication Data

On life and other paradoxes ; aphorisms and little
stories from Bert Hellinger. / translated with an introduction
by Ralph Metzner

    p. cm.
    ISBN 1-891944-89-4 (alk. paper)

Published by

ZEIG, TUCKER & THEISEN, INC.
3614 North 24th Street
Phoenix, AZ 85016

Manufactured in the United States of America

10 9 8 7 6 5 4 3 2 1

Table of Contents

APHORISMS AND LITTLE STORIES

Perceiving What Is

The Greater Power

Good and Evil

Men and Women

Helping and Healing

Life and Death

Finally ...

STATEMENTS OF EMPOWERMENT

Preliminary Comments

Honoring and Loving

Concluding Comments

Introduction & Appreciation

Ralph Metzner

Bert Hellinger is widely regarded as one of the most influential, provocative, and effective psychotherapists working in the German-speaking world today. His development as a teacher and healer is a fascinating story of self-transformation. After working for almost two decades as a priest and missionary with the South African Zulus, he converted from a religious to a psychological approach to human problems. He then immersed himself in the study of the major forms of psychotherapy, including psychoanalysis, primal therapy, Gestalt therapy, transactional analysis, hypnotherapy, and family systems therapy. He is what is called in German a *Seelsorger,* a "caretaker of souls," one who ministers to people's deepest spiritual questions and difficulties. Working at the interface of psychotherapy and spirituality, he dares to go where most psychotherapists or clergy will not, to the most basic issues of birth and death, illness and incest, suicide and genocide. He is the wisest man I know.

Using his unique development of the method of family constellations, Bert Hellinger has been able to help many thousands of individuals and families come to a greater degree of freedom from constricting entanglements with ancestral patterns, and thereby achieve a more harmonious family life. Although he scrupulously avoids all theorizing about underlying dynamics, he has, in the course of his practical healing work, formulated some startling yet cogent insights into the functioning of family systems. His observations and his methods of working with family constellations are described in detail in dozens of books and training videos. In the present volume, he has given us some of the distilled essence of his many years of practice and observation, in the forms of brief jewel-like aphorisms and epigrams, little stories, and the affirmations he calls "statements of power."

Here the *Seelsorger* has become a *Wahrsager,* a "truth-speaker" or "soothsayer" — in the literal meaning of the Old English "sooth" as "truth." To hear the truth spoken, it was believed, had a soothing effect on the anxious or tormented soul — and so do these sayings and stories open one to a calm, compassionate, and balanced perspective on the often disturbing vagaries of human existence. Furthermore, his observations and aphorisms are often tinged with a kind of wry humor, an ironic detachment, that particularly loves to deflate any pretensions to spiritual or moral superiority.

A wise person relates to pure truth like a cow relates to a barbed wire fence: as long as there is something to eat, she'll keep her distance; when not, she'll look for a gap.

In the method of family constellations, the individual is invited by the therapist to select representatives for the major figures in his or her family of origin and present situation. These representatives are then placed, silently and intuitively, without instructions, in particular positions on the central stage. Then everyone sits down and waits. After what are sometimes long, silent minutes, Hellinger may ask the representatives what they are feeling — and their responses appear to reflect in an uncanny way the realities of the individual's family situation. Hellinger may then suggest to the representatives a different positioning in relationship to each other — all of this done without any verbal interpretations or discussions. When a certain positioning is found, there is often a visible, perceptible, relief and relaxation on the part of the representatives, as well as the observing audience members. Here Hellinger has found, or brought to light, what he calls the hidden order or hidden symmetry of the family system — one of his central and most original concepts. Without an acknowledgment and expression of this order, love cannot flow freely in the family system — contrary to the common belief that one need only love enough and all problems are solved.

When I first read Bert Hellinger's statements regarding the functioning of this ordering principle, akin to but distinct from what is generally called love, I was reminded of something I had learned from my teacher of Agni ("Light-Fire Energy") Yoga, Russell Schofield. He taught that there is a love energy that is the personal love associated with the heart and its sentiments, with feeling and with healing; and there is a different kind of "love" energy that is not sentimental at all, but is rather an all-inclusive, ordering, organizing, harmonizing power. I believe this distinction parallels what Hellinger is saying.

> *Order gathers, love flows.*
> *Order and love work together.*

Some people, including some psychologists and helping professionals, have reacted strongly against this notion of order, as if Hellinger were somehow imposing a Germanic need for *Ordnung* on the fluid, ever-changing dynamics of family systems. Yet this is far from the truth. The order spoken of is an intrinsic, inherent order, often unnoticed at first until it is brought to light. One of the elements of a family system's intrinsic order, Hellinger states, is that every member of the family, including those who have died, or have been aborted, or have been excluded or rejected because of immorality, abuse, or criminality, must be acknowledged for the place they occupy, the role they have played.

Intrinsic order is the acknowledgment of limits.

The intrinsic order of a family system is often hidden or concealed from everyone, a kind of family secret, precisely because events have occurred, one or two generations back, evoking guilt, shame, anguish, rage, hatred, and the like. Once these patterns are brought to light, and the underlying feelings acknowledged, then the web of entanglements lifts, and the system re-orders and harmonizes itself in a mysterious way.

As the sounding song submits to the harmonies
so does love submit to the intrinsic order.

When the underlying order, or truth, or reality, is acknowledged, then the distorting effects of negative emotional judgments fall away, and one can perceive what is. "Acknowledging what is" became a kind of recurrent motto for Hellinger, who also used it for the title of one of his books.

Multigenerational patterns was one of the areas where I observed what was for me a remarkable congruence between

Hellinger's work and my own. In my work with shamanic and alchemical methods of inducing deep, expanded states of consciousness, for the purpose of self-understanding and transformation, I had come to guide people to encounter and dialogue with the spirits of their deceased ancestors and other relatives, releasing old patterns of confusion and alienation, bringing about a great sense of continuity and support in a familial lineage and tradition, reestablishing connections of guidance and counsel. The meetings with the "spirits of the ancestors" (to use the traditional language of indigenous people) taking place in the interior fields of consciousness were similar in essence to the meetings with the embodied representatives of deceased ancestors during Hellinger's practice of the method of family constellations. The representatives, I realized, were functioning exactly like what in a traditional society, one that acknowledges the continuity of life after death, would call a "medium." If Hellinger called the representatives' task "mediumistic," however, it probably would not work — because concepts of inadequacy would prevent it.

Hellinger discovered, using the method of family constellations, that very often a sick, suicidal, or depressed child may be unknowingly acting out of the hidden order in a multigenerational network. For example, a suicidally depressed young person may be inwardly saying to an ill or dying parent or grandparent, "Rather I die than you." The underlying systemic ordering needs to be acknowledged consciously, and when it is, when the right statement is found that expresses it, then the individual is freed from the entanglements of the past, and empowered to move on with life. This is why Hellinger calls the statements he has the representatives speak, authentically, from the heart, "statements of power."

When working with a Jewish woman in England who had lost 13 members of her family in her parents' and grandparents' generation during the Holocaust, Hellinger had her select representatives for each of them. He then had her bow, slowly and respectfully, before the representative of each one in turn, acknowledging their life and death, and asking for their blessing. At the end of this profoundly moving ceremony of reconciliation, the woman was visibly lightened and freed from an enormous burden of "survivor guilt."

In recent years, Hellinger's work has often moved into the area of healing the consequences of war, genocide, and large-scale patterns of destructiveness and hatred, in such countries as Argentina and Israel, as well as Germany. He speaks of the movements of the "family soul," which is larger than the individual: and the movements of an even larger collective soul, of which people can sense themselves to be parts.

In the soul, the shadow provides the energy for the light.

I have seen him set up a constellation with (representatives for) seven unknown victims of the Holocaust, and the seven unknown perpetrators who killed them, and the one who gave the orders. The representatives in such a constellation often seem to tap into and express profoundly healing insghts into the human condition. The individual may find peace in humbly recognizing the significance of otherwise incomprehensible and unforgivable actions, through sensing their embeddedness in a larger systemic order.

Hellinger often uses an expression that was also a favorite of Martin Heidegger's: the wonderful German word *Gelassenheit,* literally meaning "letting-be-ness." Its feeling is something like "serenity," although there is no exact English equivalent.

> *Experience is meaningful when one leaves it behind.*
> *Letting means: moving on, transformed.*

When we can let something or someone be, we can stop judging, explaining, moralizing, imposing our concepts and interpretations, and instead perceive and acknowledge what really is, and thereby open up the possibilities of transformation. *We are released from evil, only when we can serenely let it go.*

The concepts of letting-be, thus perceiving what is, and in this way transcending the dualities of "judgmentalism," are very reminiscent of Taoist and Zen Buddhist teachings. The ever-changing flow of water was for the Taoist sages both a metaphor for the natural way to live, the *Tao*, and emblematic of the desirable way to act. "Water is the softest thing in the world, but it overcomes stone, the hardest." It is both nourishing, the highest good, and it always sinks humbly to the lowest point. In the words of the *Hsin Hsin Ming*, by Sengstan, the third Zen patriarch, "If you wish to see the truth, then hold no opinions for or against anything."

Hellinger's sayings about the intrinsic order are reminiscent of another teaching of the ancient Chinese sages, namely the concept of *li*, which played an important part in both Confucian and Taoist thought. For the Taoists, according to Alan Watts, "*li* may be understood as organic order, as distinct from mechanical or legal order." In Confucius' thought, which is much more concerned with human relations in the family and society, *li* is often translated as "rite" or "propriety," the right way to do a sacrifice ritual, the right relationship between parents and children. "Without *li* humanity, righteousness, and morality cannot be achieved ... correct relationships of rulers and ministers, superiors and inferiors, fathers and sons ... cannot be achieved," says the *Records of Rites*, a Confucian classic. Confucian texts have explicit guidelines for the appropriate relationships between a first wife and a second wife, for example; just as Hellinger points out, there is a definite ordering principle at work for the relationship between former and present partners.

In pointing to some similarities between Hellinger's teachings and those of the old Chinese philosophers, I do not mean to imply that he derived his philosophy from these writings. It is one of the remarkable features of his work that he is resolutely committed to the empiricism of phenomenology: that is, all of this statements are offered as observations made in the practice of family systems therapy, not as generalizable principles or truths. The "statements of empowerment" are not prescriptions, to be applied by rote; they were observed to be empowering, bringing about a resolution, in particular situations.

To those who would challenge his statements, Hellinger simply refers to his observations. The inherent order, he says, is not an opinion that one can have or change, at will. "It is not thought up, it is discovered." The philosophical similarities to other teachings can function to clarify and deepen our understanding of some of these deepest paradoxes and mysteries of human existence.

In some ways, Bert Hellinger, and the role he plays at the interface of psychotherapy and spiritual teaching, reminds me of the 13th century Dominican priest, theologian, mystic, and preacher, Meister Eckhart. Eckhart was renowned as a

charismatic *Seelsorger*, who emerged from the rarified intel-
lectual atmosphere of the theological colleges, with its dis-
courses in Latin, to become an itinerant priest, preaching in
German to ordinary people, applying his mystical insights
and theological learning to the problems of living a life in-
spired by divinity. He particularly committed himself to aid-
ing and counseling the communities of nuns, such as the Beg-
ines, who were often the targets of considerable opprobrium
on the part of the ecclesiastical hierachy.

A final suggestive parallel between Eckhart and Hellinger
is in their use and mastery of the German language. Eckhart's
German sermons owe much of their powerful impact to the
way he condenses complex thoughts into short, often colorful, phrases that are close to poetry. In German, the word for
poetry, *Dichtung*, is an alchemical metaphor; it literally
means "condensation." In a poem, a *Gedicht*, thoughts and
images are packed into compact and memorable form. For
this linguistic reason, Hellinger's original title for this little
book — *Verdichtetes* — presented an insurmountable problem
for the translator. The Greek-derived word *aphorism*, which
refers to limits and boundaries, will have to serve to convey
these gems of philosophical insight to the English-speaking
reader.

Author's Preface

Dear Reader,

The sayings and little stories collected here have a place in the practice of living. That is to say, they arose in the course of therapeutic work, while searching for a resolution; or, in the course of a conversation with friends, a hitherto hidden connection may suddenly have appeared. The particular occasions on which the connections became apparent may still be recalled and should be considered, if one wishes to comprehend their sense and purpose. However, they also transcend the particular, and it could lead to misunderstanding were one to limit them to the specific occasions.

Some of these sayings and stories are perhaps at first confusing, because they contradict our usual concepts of reason and logic. But if we let them work on us, we may find in them a kind of meaning that transcends the usual boundaries — meaning that cannot be made clearer through explanation, or dissolved through contradiction; and thus we are captivated.

In addition, this book contains a collection of what I call "statements of empowerment." They were spoken for particular clients in the course of family constellation psychotherapy, and then repeated by them, with heartfelt concentration, to the representatives of their parents or other family members. In such statements, there is a condensation of healing speech and deed. Where someone is trapped in another's fate or in personal guilt, they can bring about a resolution. They express the recognition of having taken something from or having done something to another human being. They permit leave-taking and liberate us for what is to come. For these statements, it is important to understand the particular situations in which they are spoken; and this is therefore indicated with each statement.

This is a book intended for contemplation. Often it will be sufficient to read only a few passages. One can also begin at any point.

I wish for you patience in the reading of this book, for the insight that reconciles the contradictions comes only with time. The fruit of that insight is then also the knowledge that heals, and the speaking and the doing.

Yours,
Bert Hellinger

Acknowledgment

My friend Dr. Norbert Linz has often listened to me reading from these sayings and stories, and he urged and persuaded me to publish them in book form. Furthermore, he helped me with the selection of texts and with their formulation. Many of the stories and sayings are, therefore, our collabora tive work.

Other friends, including Dr. Otto Brink, Dr. Robert Langlotz, Jakob and Sieglinde Schneider, and Dr. Gunthard Weber, have read proofs of the book and have made impor tant suggestions for changes.

To all of them I offer my heartfelt thanks.

Bert Hellinger

APHORISMS AND LITTLE STORIES

Perceiving What Is

Introductory Comments

When we wish to grasp a delicate object, we take hold of it between thumb and index finger. The two fingers are opposed to one another, and so they "grasp" what lies between them and yet is totally separate and different from them. Our situation is sometimes quite similar with regard to words and their meaning.

Therefore, we must often adopt multiple perspectives on essential questions. Wholeness is inclusive, not exclusive, and even the opposite then appears as one part among many, complementing but not displacing the other parts.

Seeing

Dim light cannot make the clear glass dimmer;
but the cloudy glass does make the bright light dimmer.

Insight comes about through consonance.

Hope muddies seeing.

Scepticism is like faith: both are substitutes for seeing.

Habit is in opposition to seeing what is new,
which for those who dare,
resolves their entanglement with the past
and frees them from its consequences.

What actually is, is indescribable;
but who sees it, knows.

To experience means perceiving what is.

We step into the sun, and already it is light.

Illumination is like many beings inclining toward a bright center.

In the bucket of water we dimly sense, without grasping it, the ocean.

Beauty requires devotion.

Readiness for seeing is opposed by, on the one hand, our habit of taking something that is bad for us as obligatory, and experiencing it as innocence; and on the other hand, our habit of regarding the seeing that shows us the solutions as betrayal of an order, and experiencing it as guilt.

Delusion

A circus acquired a polar bear. But since it only needed him for exhibition, he was locked in a cage. The cage was so narrow that the bear could not even turn around in it — and so he only took two paces forward and two paces backwards.

After many years, the circus took pity on the polar bear and sold him to a zoo. There he found himself in a large field. Yet he only walked two paces forward and two paces backwards. When another polar bear asked him: "Why are you doing this?" he replied: "Because I was locked for a long time in a cage."

In this way a past misfortune becomes, through habit, the accepted order of things; and the inner image of an outer restriction from the past distorts our seeing of the spaciousness in the present. Then habit functions like conscience: instead of seeing what is, we substitute an inner image of what is already past, as though it were still present.

Thinking

Intuition is always sudden,
only thinking takes a long time.

What can be thought is mostly false.

A concept is to reality as a tangent is to a sphere.
It can touch the sphere but not encompass it.
However, a word such as "Earth" has weight.

Order is a river that flows.

Growth always deviates a little bit.

A theory at best points in a direction, but it can be neither
path nor goal.

Practice disturbs theory.

The essential is easy and light; so is the true.

At the boundary we arrive at insight.

Decisions are provisional.

The moment is my boundary.

The direct path sometimes takes longer.

Often the inner picture comes about only by hearsay and
thus creates an order based solely on presuppositions. Then
we have hearsay instead of seeing, belief instead of knowledge, and arbitrariness instead of truth.

Curiosity

A man asked his friend: "Do you understand anything about possession?" The friend answered: "Perhaps — but what are you really concerned about?"

"I went with my wife to a psychic, who told her she was possessed by the devil. What should I do now?"

The friend answered: "If you go to such a person, you get what you deserve. Now you are possessed by an inner image that you won't be able to get rid of so easily. Did you hear about Hernando Cortez? With a couple of hundred soldiers, he conquered the immense empire of the Aztecs. Do you know how he was able to do that? He didn't know what the others thought."

Knowing

Illumination is knowing the intrinsic order.

Belief demands that we deny what we know — and what we don't know.

We can only have "great" ideas with our eyes closed.

A know-it-all doesn't need much knowledge.

Pure truth is a matter of lies.

A wise person relates to pure truth like a cow relates to a barbed wire fence: as long as there is something to eat, she'll keep her distance; when not, she'll look for a gap in the fence.

The intrinsic order is overwhelming.

The right thing is hard to find and easy to understand.

In preparing to find something, we often have to renounce something.

Self-confidence is knowing your own way.

What is right does not need to be defended; the same goes for what is not right.

Having followers reduces freedom.

Meaning

I become cautious when you agree with me, because perhaps you only have an opinion.
If you had perceived, your perception would have been different from mine.

Letting go of an opinion is a gain;
letting go of an insight is a loss.

A false impression leaves its mark on whoever has it.

Everyone is his own jackass.

To argue means:
playing in a sandbox while underneath a vein of gold lies hidden.

Sometimes a commentary has the same effect as a can of water on a drop of wine.

Explanation substitutes for understanding; if you have understood, you can describe.

Confusion is related to fullness; only the small is clear.

Life flows past the debates of the experts.

With the right thing, there is no choice.

The intrinsic order cannot be manipulated.

The Consequences

One friend showed another a new high wall and said: "Look, I built this myself!"

The friend agreed: "Yes, it's completely your own work. And if you now run up against it, the wall will remain standing."

The Dream

Someone awakens from a dream, and because he feels it is significant, wants to write it down. Then he realizes: "If I try to remember or interpret the dream, its power will be lost."

Heaven and Earth

In the vicinity of Cologne, somewhere in the Bergenland, there lived two eccentric farmers, each one alone on his farm; and though they were neighbors, neither wanted anything to do with the other. They maintained their boundaries with exactness, one never permitting the other to enter his territory. One of them cultivated only potatoes, for, as he said, the nourishing fruit thrives in the dark womb of the earth. The other one planted only apple trees, for, as he maintained, the blessings of the delicious fruit only come from above. So each one used his land in his own way, each one convinced that his was the only right way. Each one's nourishment corresponded to his cultivation.

After many years, they were both invited, without knowing of one another, to the same wedding, and each one brought what he had — the one brought potatoes, the other apples. The young couple was appreciative of the offerings, and so, at the wedding feast, both were served, one after the other, beautifully cooked and prepared, the potatoes salted and the apples sweetened. However, something seemed to be amiss, for the guests had long faces. There was so much disquiet in the hall that the bride could stand it no longer. She jumped up and said, "Wait a minute, I'm going to bring something better."

She took the potatoes and the apples back into the kitchen, threw them together into a pot, added some spices, cooked it once more, and presented it as a new dish.

Although it took a little while before the wedding guests ventured to try the new dish, their surprise was great when they realized how good it tasted. From that time on, people eat potatoes and apples mixed together in the Rhineland, and this dish from above and below is called "Heaven and Earth."

The two eccentric farmers each continued in his own way of doing things.

Acting

Dry runs are not sufficient for insight;
only those who dive in know what is dangerous and what is supportive.

Liking certain music doesn't mean we can play it.

In the process of acting, I receive a gift.

Something that may be hidden to curiosity can be comprehended through acting.

What is true has to prove itself.

One handles life's difficulties like children handle deep water: they learn to swim.

Some people deal with a problem as if it were the cause of its solution.

The further away you push something, the larger it becomes.

Those who look for reasons often seek excuses.

The problem is heavy; the solution is light.

The pike does not catch the whole swarm, only a single fish.

Power

An elite troop of American police officers admitted only the very best recruits, but never more than 99 altogether. They always performed their duties alone. Once when there was an uprising in a prison, one of the officers went there and single-handedly put it down. Afterwards, someone asked him: "How did you do that?" "Quite simply," he replied, "I was right."

The Lingerer

A prisoner breaks out of jail, is pursued, and comes to a river and has to cross it. He takes his shoes off, tests the water with his naked toe, and says, "That's too cold for me."

His pursuers catch up to him — he is shot to death.

Holding Still

Some run after good fortune,
not realizing that good fortune is running after them,
but never reaches them,
because they are running.

With blinders on, one runs faster.

Whoever goes to bed with the chickens never sees the stars.

Wisdom wakes.

If the decision were ripe, you would know it.

The wrong way is endless.

Truth is protected.

Just because someone asks a question does not give that person the right to an answer.

When something is right, no explanation is required.

No answer is required when the motive behind the question is malicious.

What we take in hand becomes small.

Recognition

A man went to war, and his weapon was a machine gun. When his troop was attacked and he wanted to fire on the enemies, his gun got stuck. Although he desperately pressed the trigger, not a single shot was fired. Then, when he could already see the whites of the eyes of his enemy, he recognized that it was a friend.

Fury

A certain Ludwig van B., in a fury over the loss of a penny, wrote a piano piece with that title. Yet the whole time the coin was lying under his piano.

The Choice

A person is walking through the bright, festively decorated streets before Christmas, when a lighted sign above a shop catches his eye: "Delicacies from Around the World." He stands still, gazing at the delicacies laid out so tastily, and his mouth begins to water. Then he clicks his tongue and says: "What I'd really like now is a piece of dry bread."

The River

What "letting be" means is revealed to those who are open to their experiences, and hidden to those who only take positions.

For the one who stands at the bank of the river, gazing at it from that position, the river rushes past. It makes little difference whether he is standing on the left or the right bank: he knows little or nothing of the river and its power.

Letting Be

Experience is meaningful when one leaves it behind.

One takes what is, temporarily.

What one holds on to, flees.

Narcissus, instead of looking out of the window, gazes into the mirror.

Insight knows its limits, and humility assents to them.

Humility has integrity.

Letting go means: moving on, transformed.

The squirrel collects so much because it forgets.

The optimum is a little bit less.

Completeness has to maintain itself within limits.

The price of beauty is a spot.

The student prefers learning to experience.

If you come upon it later, you will have learned it better.

Clearing Out

A man lived in a small house, and over the years, a lot of stuff accumulated in his rooms. Guests would bring their things with them, and when they left, they would leave quite a few bags behind. It was as if they were still there, although they had long since moved on forever.

Also, whatever the owner himself collected remained in the house. Nothing was to be left in the past or lost. Even broken things still held memories, and therefore stayed, and continued to take up space.

Only when the owner was almost choking did he begin to clear things out. He started with his books. Did he still want to contemplate the old images, or understand the strange teachings and stories? Whatever was completed he removed from his house; and in the rooms it became light and bright.

Then he opened the bags of the guests to see if there was anything that he could use. During this process, he discovered a few treasures, and laid them aside. The rest he took outside.

He threw all the old stuff into a deep pit, covered it neatly with earth, and then sowed grass over it.

Fullness Draws
Away from the Small

Whoever looks for the hair misses the soup.

Instead of squinting into the sun, some do it into the shadows.

Some who make an objection are taking a single stone from the cathedral, and finding it is nothing special.

Holding fast to the narrow is to refuse development.

An objection works on the grass like a scythe: it dies before seeding.

Conspicuous means: to be noticed because of appearances.

If you confront the first objection, you do not need to bow to the second.

Only multitudes are immeasurable; fullness has measure.

Fullness does not defend itself against anything.

Fear means: I hold onto the small instead of the great.

Narrowness

One warm summer's day, a man comes to a peaceful lake. He climbs into a boat, rows out onto the water, and has a feeling of the fullness of life. Then he pulls out a thimble, takes a little water, and examines it closely with a magnifying glass. So time passes.

He could have, instead, gone into the water, and let himself be carried by it.

Wisdom

A wise person assents to the world as it is, without fear and without purpose.

A wise one is reconciled to impermanence and does not strive to transcend that which dissolves in death.

Wise ones are able to maintain an overview, because they are in harmony; they only intervene when the flow of life requires it.

The wise one can discern whether something will work or not, because he does not have an agenda.

Wisdom is the fruit of long discipline and exercise; however, when you have it, it's effortless.

Wisdom is always moving on the path, and arriving at the goal without seeking it.

Wisdom grows.

The Greater Power

Introductory Observation

Pure truth seems bright to us,
but, like the Full Moon,
it conceals a dark side.
It blinds us with its brightness

Thus the more we attempt to grasp or assert
the side turned toward us,
the greater our perplexity,
as the hidden side secretly
eludes our understanding.

That Which Is Concealed

For some, religion consists of an image of God, constructed by a fearful heart in its own likeness, so that it won't be annihilated.

Or:

Religion is a wave that lifts us up and throws us on a distant shore:

against this current there is no going back.

Myths can deceive us with images of brightness where darkness prevails; and they may show us darkness where everything is open for one who perceives.

The images that are effective are also obscure.

Bright images and myths are part of the darkness of the Spirit, which the hero on his journey must overcome, so that he won't lose his head.

Great secrets do not need to be protected: they preserve themselves.

Theology attempts to uncover the mystery and thereby turns it into an object;

science sometimes does the same with nature, and psychology with the soul.

The secret uncovered avenges itself.

Sometimes the last word is silence.

Emptiness

The disciples of a teacher abandon him, and as they make their way back home, they ask one another soberly: "What were we looking for with him?"

One of them remarks:

"Blindly we stepped into a carriage, drawn by blind horses, with a blind coachman, moving blindly onwards. If we were to proceed on our own, with a staff, like blind men, feeling our way, we might begin to sense, as we stand at the edge of the abyss, with our staff, the nothingness."

Zeal

The faith that binds a group together hinders it from loving other groups.

Freedom of religion frees me from the faith of others; just as freedom of conscience frees me from the conscience of others.

The followers of Yahweh are filled with zeal.

To want something eternal is to want something terrible.

Many pious people say: You must not have any god besides me.

A zealot is like a scarab beetle that believes that with his little hind legs he turns the world.

What you fight for does not remain; what you fight against, you can't get rid of.

The god that we create lies to us.

For some, religion is a kind of striving that lacks true devotion.

Devotion is without purpose.

If you know it, then we may as well be silent about it.

Happiness is found by one who bends.

Expectation

A motorcyclist, proud owner of a heavy machine, stopped at a parking lot, where he discovered a small spot on the exhaust pipe. He took a cloth and carefully rubbed the spot clean. Observing this, a passerby remarked: "When you take care of this machine with such devotion, it will bless you."

Fire

The story is told of Prometheus that he stole fire from the gods to give to humankind.

The gods allowed him to do this, but then he found himself chained to a rock.

What he did not know was that the gods would have given fire to humans willingly.

The Earth

Not Heaven, but Earth is the measure.

Heaven separates us, whereas Earth carries us.

Although for many the world stands in opposition to the love of God, true reverence for it is actually proof of that love.

Gazing heavenward, we gaze at emptiness.

Religion is loving participation in an ever-greater wholeness.

We are in the soul, not the soul in us.

Phenomenology is openness to the divine.

Beauty is inconceivable, yet compelling.

Peacefulness means: to pulsate with the Earth.

Gathering can only take place within boundaries.

The rain falling from the sky seeks many streams on the way to the ocean.

I see your star, and follow mine.

A Better Way

A young man from a rich family went to a far-off country. There he gambled away his inheritance. When he had lost everything, he went to work for a farmer.

His brother did exactly the same. When he too had gambled away his inheritance, he came to the same farmer.

Now both brothers reflected within themselves. One brother said: "When I think back to our home, and how well the people working for our father lived, I'm drawn to return to him. I will say to my father, 'I've done everything wrong. Please take me back and let me be as one of your servants.'"

The other brother replied: "I'm going to do something different. Tomorrow I will look for better work, I will save a little fortune, marry a daughter of these lands, and live here just as the others."

The Giveaway

What in earlier times were known as devotion and adoration
are both a kind of releasing or relinquishing:
accepting everything as it comes, giving everything as required — with love.

Mysticism develops when the parents are missing.

Ascetics lack their mother; addicts lack their father.

We shouldn't hold it against Jesus that the rich young man
went away from him with sadness.

Stillness comes from the calm yielding to that which carries
us.

A calling means: a power takes us in its service, and if we resist, we wither.

We complain that God has withdrawn from the world. He
has also withdrawn from the Bible.

To the God who has withdrawn, we must not pray.

That which is last is at the beginning, and the beginning is
now.

Dependence

A man acquired a sheep, and thereby became a shepherd. Whenever he said anything to the sheep, it answered with a "baah." The shepherd was happy.

As the sheep grew somewhat older, it attacked the shepherd angrily whenever he said anything. The shepherd thought: "I've never been so deeply bonded with my sheep."

Later, when the sheep was even older, it simply walked away.

Then the shepherd became sad, for now he was just an ordinary man again.

Good and Evil

Introductory Comments

When one becomes indignant over a bad situation, one appears to be on the side of good and against evil, on the side of justice and opposed to injustice. One intervenes between perpetrator and victim in order to prevent further evil. However, one could also come between them with love, and that would surely be better. So what do the indignant ones want? What are they really acomplishing?

The indignant ones conduct themselves as if they were themselves victims, although they are not. They assume the right to demand reparation from the perpetrator, although no injustice has been done to them. They assume the role of advocate for the victims, as if the victims had given them the right to represent them; in doing so, they leave the real victims without rights.

And what do the indignant ones do with this pretension? They take the liberty of doing bad things to the perpetrators, without fear of any bad consequences for their own person; since their bad deeds appear in the light of the good, they do not fear any punishment. In order to maintain their justified indignation, such people dramatize both the injustice suffered by the victims, and the consequences of the guilty deed. They intimidate the victim into seeing the injustice in the same way as they do. Otherwise the victims might themselves become suspect and the targets of righteous indignation, as if they were themselves perpetrators.

From the perspective of indignation, it is difficult for victims to let go of their suffering, and perpetrators to let go of their guilt. If victims and perpetrators are allowed to find resolution and reconciliation in their own way, they may permit themselves and each other a new beginning. But if righteous indignation enters into the picture, such a resolution is more difficult, since the indignant ones are generally not satisfied until the perpetrator has been completely destroyed and humiliated, even if this intensifies the suffering of the victims.

Indignation is in the first place a question of morality. That is to say, here one is not concerned with helping another being, but rather with a certain demand, for which the indignant ones see and present themselves as executors. Therefore, in contrast to someone who loves, such a person knows neither compassion nor restraint.

Morality

A moralist is someone who applies a small measuring instrument to the great world.

For the moralist, "good" means, "I have more rights than you," and "evil" means, "You have fewer rights than I do."

What we designate as good is often only what is convenient.

A knife-thrower is far from being a surgeon.

Whoever wants to improve another, becomes worse himself.

We are released from evil only when we can serenely let it go.

Better people are lonely.

We are often opposed to the things we secretly desire.

That which we have thoroughly reviled will be left to us as our reward.

Many principles, if they have a price at all, turn out to be quite cheap.

The uplifted index finger can also be bent.

Whoever judges, participates.

Indignation

The bull is blinded by his red cloth.

Where there is one innocent, there are more evil ones than before.

Indignant ones judge both victims and perpetrators, as if they had the right to do so.

When one feels righteous, one is already wrong.

The innocent fool is not against anything.

When victims become indignant, their transformation is delayed or lost.

Indignation has never made anyone pure.

Rejection leads to resemblance.

Triumph is insufficient for happiness.

Only what we love lets us be free.

The light that warms and glows does not need to consume all the wood in the world.

The wound heals more easily under a Band-Aid.

Revenge

A retail merchant wrote the following letter to his wholesale supplier:

Dear Sirs,

Four weeks ago, I ordered a box of soap. It has still not arrived. My supply is sold out, and because of your omission, I am suffering major losses. But I suppose us little guys just have to put up with the fact that you big boys treat us like dirt.

And so the letter continued, for several pages. Then, under the signature, there followed a postscript:

P.S. In the meantime, I have found the box of soap.

The Little Tailor

Do you know how the brave little guy evaded the attack of the unicorn?

He stepped aside a little.

Guilt

Guilt is for the soul what pain is for the body.

In the soul, the shadow provides the energy for the light.

Without guilt there can be no transformation.

Often the greatest treasures are protected by a dragon.

Greatness is always wrapped in imperfection.

Greed means: wanting to have, but not accepting.
Humility means to accept with love.

The one best able to resolve conflicts by peaceful means is the strongest.

Only in drinking the wine do we know its effect.

In desire is revealed the deep sustenance of the world.

There are two groups of sinners:
so-called evil-doers, and
those who wish them ill.
The second group is called "the just ones."

Loving one's enemy is insight.

The Spell

There are stories that intimidate and delude us, so that we do not dare to perceive what is happening in reality. Something like that happens to children when they hear the story of the stork; and something similar may have happened to those delivered to the death camp when they read over the entrance: "Labor makes us free."

But once in a while, someone comes along who has the courage to look at the reality and to break the spell. Like the little child who, in the crowd of excited people around the idolized dictator, pointed and loudly and clearly said what everyone knew, but no one dared to admit to themselves or say out loud, "But he is naked!"

Or like the musician who stood at the side of the road when the rat catcher passed by with a whole group of children following him. He played a different rhythm, which served to bring some of the children out of step.

The Wish

An older woman greatly feared intruders. Every evening she looked under the bed and in the wardrobe to see if there might be an intruder hiding.

When, after many years, she really found an intruder under her bed, she said, "At last!"

Conscience

For the conscience, loyalty carries more weight than truth.

What conscience tells us is an interpretation.

Without insight, conscience is blind.

Insight overcomes the fear of guilt.

Often the good thing comes about only through a transgression.

The good resulting from insight releases what conscience has bound
— and binds, where conscience releases.

Justice often means:
the happiness of the many has to yield to the revenge of a few.

Conscience sows discord.

Conscience is not good; it must become good.

Conscience is hard; mildness transgresses.

Only those who arrive at the border may cross it:
otherwise, they are children playing at being married.

On Freedom

Question: "What shall I do? My parents still meddle in every-thing."

Answer: "Your parents can meddle, and you can do what you think is right."

On Memory

There are stories that are like fences. They restrict us and im-prison us. If we comply, they offer us security, and when we want to go further, they block our way.

We sometimes tell ourselves such stories and call them me-mories. Memory then becomes a shackle, and our space for expres-sion becomes limited.

On Risk

A long time ago, a man was held prisoner in a palace, in which, according to legend, there was also a labyrinth; often he would creep past a certain dark portal, which, it was said, led to destruc-tion.

He heard that many people had broken through the door by force, but none had returned; and thus the fear of those who re-mained behind grew stronger and stronger.

But the prisoner inspected the doorway very closely. Then, one night, when all the guards were asleep, he decisively made his way through the dark portal — and stood outside.

Innocence

Whiteness attracts blemishes.

Most angels are fallen ones.

Ever since the Fall, innocence has been difficult.

Innocence sometimes is merely that which one has imagined, as opposed to that which is.

Purification is also taking leave from innocence.

A little bit of sin is helpful for virtue.

Good is what is required by life as the next step.

Some people eat pork chops, because others butcher the pigs for them.

A thing is not bad just because I desire it.

For purification, everyone has to glow for himself.

It often happens that what we forgive ends up in our own backpack.

Reconciliation means: I leave you in peace.

Settling the Accounts

A man gets up one morning with a heavy heart, for he knows that this is the day his creditors are coming, and he has to settle up with them. He realizes he still has a little time, so he goes to his shelves, picks up the first folder, and looks into the records. There he finds the invoices he still has to pay. He inspects them closely and finds some that are overbillings, some that are for services promised but never carried out, and others for goods that were ordered but never delivered. He considers what is just and right, and decides to be on the lookout for inappropriate charges. Then he closes that folder and picks up the second one.

Here he finds lists of services received for which he believes himself to be heavily indebted. But at the end of these lists there are notations such as "gratis," "already paid," or "complimentary." He recalls images of people who were dear and precious to him, and his heart becomes wide and warm. Then he closes the second folder too, and picks up a third.

In this one, he finds offers that he solicited in order to acquire things that had been necessary for some time. But at the end of the list of offers is the notation: "pre-payment only." Here he knows that he will require additional time in order to check on the reliability of these offers. So he closes this third folder as well, and puts it back on the shelf.

Then his creditors arrive, and when they have taken their places, they fill the room with their presence. Yet no one says anything.

In seeing them all in front of him like this, he becomes oddly lighthearted, as if everything that was so confusing has now become comprehensible; he feels that he has the power to settle up with them and that he will do it.

As he is waiting, his inner image assumes a certain order. He now knows for sure which of the creditors must be addressed first, which next, and so on. He shares his image with the creditors, thanks them for coming, and assures them that, in due course, he will settle up with each of them. They all agree and leave, and only one of the creditors remains, the one with whom he wants to settle up right away.

The two men lay everything out between them. They know the time for haggling is over, and now it's time to close the deal, and since both are serious about it, they quickly come to an agreement. But as the creditor gets up to leave, he turns around one more time and says: "I'll give you another little grace period."

Men and Women

On Love

To show esteem to one of the other gender means:
to let oneself be gifted by the other,
and yet to respect his or her mystery.

In relationship to the sex of the other:
instead of wanting to possess it, honor it.

Curiosity destroys intimacy.

In respecting the dignity of the other, I preserve myself.

In releasing my hold on my self,
I also give up fear of you.

One who knows, avoids making declarations of never-ending love:
this person knows about leaving and ending,
and prefers to love with that in mind.

Tristan and Isolde: the deepest Yes and the deepest No.

I give to you also the renouncing of you — with love.

Freedom is part of commitment.

Even when it does not remain,
it's beautiful that it was.

Intrinsic Order

Obligation belongs with freedom,
as limits belong with fullness.

Without commitment there can be no freedom —
for to what should the freedom be related?

Intrinsic order is the acknowledgment of limits.

Some seek the great freedom:
but instead of arriving in a green meadow,
they end up in the zoo.

A fish may jump out of the water:
but of what use is that
if it chokes on fresh air?

If one is content,
one will have more of what one already has.

Good fortune at the expense of others generally lasts only a
short time.

When the stags leave,
the cows remain.

Even if you leave, our love remains.

The Hare and the Hedgehog

"Do you know the fairy tale about the hare and the hedgehog?"

"Yes, the hare wanted to have a race, and so overexerted himself that he died."

"Do you also know how this happened? He could not distinguish between man and woman."

Briar Rose

Briar Rose pierced herself with a spindle, collapsed and fell into a deep sleep.

Then the nurse took the spindle, pricked Briar Rose a second time, and she woke up.

The nurse said: "You must take the spindle and prick yourself a third time."

Briar Rose did as she was told. Then her cheeks became red, and among the thorns surrounding the castle, there bloomed roses.

The Wolf and the Seven Kids

The nanny goat said to her seven kids: "Beware of the bad wolf."

Translated, this means: "Beware of the bad father."

In other words, the wolf is the billy goat, who after separation from his mate, is denied access to his children.

The solution: the older kids go with the father, the youngest stays with the mother.

The Prince

"Do you know how one transforms a frog into a prince? Not like in the fairy tale, of course."

"At the moment, I have no idea."

"I can give the answer: You have to kiss the frog."

Courage

*Do you know the fairy tale about the man who set out to learn
what fear was?*

   Do you know where he finally learned it?
   In bed with a woman.

Helping and Healing

Caution

For some, the experience of psychotherapy is like the story of the stone of Sisyphus:
when it finally does get to the top, it just lies there.

Avoiding something brings it about.

Ambivalence means: neither the one nor the other.

A premonition signifies a secret intention.

Even remaining where you are is a transformation.

Those who have stayed young are often those who have stayed still.

Often, time may squander essence, just like the search for knowledge squanders truth.

Grace passes by.

A rebel refuses to be an equal.

The right place is never given as a gift; it is taken.

At times, melancholy is a cover for happiness.

The sea of tears is small.

Trust

The psychotherapist may put up a new sail, but it is the same wind that blows.

In order to drive out the devil, you first have to paint him on the wall.

How can something wilt as it continues to grow?

Parents have no shadow side.

Love is assent to whatever grows.

The healing image is found, not developed.

The specific weight of the soul is equal to the sum of what has been dared.

Compassion requires the courage to face all of the suffering.

In order to bring about peace, you need the blessing of a sinner.

If you can't solve the problem yourself, make room for the master.

I take my dandelion and blow, and one year later, on many a meadow there blooms many more beautiful flowers.

On Duration

An employee said to her boss: "I'm having a hard time. I have started psychotherapy, and the therapist told me the psychotherapy would take five years."

The boss answered: "He told you that it would take five years for you to feel better. No wonder you're feeling bad."

On Warmth

In the spring, some children came into the forest and found a snowman. But because the sun was shining, his face was distorted as if he were crying. The children caressed him, because they wanted to help him, but with the touch of their warm little hands, his size dwindled even further.

When they looked for him later, they found delicate spring wildflowers where the snowman had been standing.

Helping

A man steps out of his house, presses through the crowds in the marketplace, passes through a narrow alley, reaches the arterial road and the intersection.

Suddenly there is a screeching of brakes, a bus starts to skid, some people scream: then he hears the crash.

He doesn't know what's happening to him: he flees, as fast as his feet will carry him, back along the arterial road and the narrow alley, through the crowds in the marketplace, he reaches his house, storms through the front door, closing it behind him, flies up the stairs to his apartment, closes the door behind him, runs along the corridor to the last, bare room, closes the door behind him — and takes a deep breath.

There he stands: having fled, locked in and alone. The shock in his limbs is so intense, that he does not dare to move. So he waits.

On the following day, his girlfriend misses him. She goes to the telephone and attempts to call him, but nobody answers. She hurries over to his house, rings the bell downstairs, but no one answers. She goes to the police, requests their assistance and returns with two officers. They open the outer door, rush up the stairs to the door of the apartment and open it, run along the corridor to the last room, knock on the door, wait a moment, and then open the door to find the man, frozen stiff with fear.

The girlfriend thanks the two officers and asks them to leave. She waits a while and then realizes that she can't accomplish anything. She promises to return the next day, and she leaves.

The following day, she finds the downstairs door open, but the apartment door still closed. She opens it, goes to the last room, opens this door and finds her friend. Since he doesn't say anything, she talks to him about what she experienced on the way over: how the sun shone through the clouds, birds sang in the branches, children played catch and the city droned on in its rhythms. She sees that she can't do anything for him this time either. She promises to return the next day, and she leaves.

The following morning, she finds the downstairs door and the apartment door open; she continues on to the last room in the corridor, enters and finds her friend, still in shock. She remains a little while and tells him about her trip to the circus the previous evening, and all the colorful spectacles she saw there, the sprightly marching band, the loud sounds, the tension as the lions entered, and the relief when everything turned out all right. She also tells him about the antics of the clown, about the noble horses with their white tassels, and about the merry throngs of people. Then, as she finishes, she promises: "I'll come back tomorrow."

The following morning, even the door to the back room stands open. However, no one comes to the door. Now, the man can no longer stand it in the house. He first closes the door to the room behind him, and then the front door of the apartment, and finally, he walks through the downstairs door out into the open. He presses through the crowd of people in the marketplace, walks through the narrow alley, reaches the arterial road, crosses the intersection — and searches with determination for his girlfriend.

Life and Death

Ending

The victory of life over death leads to the desolation of the Earth.

To do something for the sake of being remembered is to attempt to outrun one's destiny.

Devotees of extreme sports have to struggle hard for their dying.

What we call immortal belongs to the past.

When the new leaf arrives, the old one falls off.

Truth wants to prolong the present moment.

Desire and aggression are both forms of resistance to death.

The hare trusts his feeling and continues eating, knowing nothing of the hunter who is aiming at him.

Looking toward the end makes it come more quickly.

Two doomed warriors are fighting fearlessly, while standing

over their graves: the victor can look forward to a double grave.

It is best to treat a joyous experience like a piece of sugar: delighting in it and letting it dissolve.

Fulfillment

In the seed form, the whole already is at work, yet without being fully present.

That which has been attained becomes effective when we let it be.

We practice the ancient way — in moving on.

In dwindling, we become full.

The lesser power lasts longer.

Now is always, and everything flows now.

The Earth builds herself from what has been.

Wisdom is ancient.

Peace-making means: allowing it to have been so;
Leave-taking means: so it was.

One wears old age like a crown.

Death guides those who follow it; and overtakes those who flee it.

The dead have time.

What is full is gone.

Meaning

In South Africa, when two Zulus meet, one will say: "I saw you. Are you still living?"

"Yes," the other will reply, "I'm still here. And you?"

"Me too, I'm also still living."

When a stranger sees a Zulu apparently doing nothing, and asks him, "Aren't you bored?" the latter replies, "I'm alive, aren't I?" For him, nothing is lacking that would give his life additional content or meaning.

We find the same attitude in a loyal follower of Konradin, the last of the Staufer dynasty, who was sitting in a prison castle, playing chess with a friend, when a messenger brought him the news that he was to be executed in one hour. He said: "Let's play on."

Finally ...

Sameness

The breeze wafts and whispers,
the storm rushes and roars.
Yet it is the same wind,
the same song.

It is the same water,
for drinking and for drowning;
it carries us and buries us.

Whatever lives, wears out,
maintains itself and destroys;
in the one as in the other,
driven by the same force.

This power counts.

Then whom do the differences serve?

STATEMENTS OF EMPOWERMENT

Preliminary Comments

Order and Love

Love fulfills that which order contains.
Love is the water, order the vessel.

Order gathers, love flows.

Order and love work together.

As the sounding song submits to the harmonies,
so does love submit to the intrinsic order.

And as the ear adjusts with difficulty to dissonance,
even when it has been explained,
so does the soul adjust with difficulty
to love without order.

Some people regard this inherent order
as if it were an opinion
that one can have or change, at will.

But the order is predestined.
It is effective, whether or not we understand it.
It is not thought up, it is discovered.
We infer the order, like the meaning and the soul,
from its effects.

Thanksgiving at the Dawning of Our Lives

Dear Mother,

I accept from you everything,
all of it, with all the trimmings,
and at the full price that you paid for it,
and that I too am paying for it.

I will make something of it,
for your pleasure, and in your memory.
It shall not have been in vain.

I will hold on to it and honor it
and when I can, I will pass it on, as you did.

I take you as my mother,
and you can have me as your child.

You are for me the right one,
and I am the right child for you.

You are the Big One, I am the Little One.
You give and I receive — Dear Mother.

I am happy that you have chosen Father.
The two of you are the right ones for me.
Only you!

Dear Father,

From you too, I accept everything,
all of it, with all the trimmings,
and at the full price that it cost you,
and which it is costing me.

I will make something of it,
for your pleasure, and in your memory.
It shall not have been for nothing.

I will hold on to it and honor it
and when I can, I will pass it on, as you did.

I take you as my father,
and you can have me as your child.

You are for me the right one,
and I am the right child for you.

You are the Big One, I am the Little One.
You give and I receive — Dear Father.

I am happy that you have chosen Mother.
The two of you are the right ones for me.
Only you!

Honoring and Loving

Men and Women

Husband and wife to each other:
I take you as my wife/as my husband/with everything that belongs with you.

Parents to each other:
In our children, I respect you and love you.

Parents of a handicapped or deceased child to each other:
We will bear it together — with love.

Husband to his wife who has died giving birth to their child:
My love for you remains; and in remembrance of you, I will take care of our child.

Husband, suffering from terminal illness, to his wife:
I entrust our children to you — with love.

Second wife, to the divorced first wife:
You are the first, I am the second.

Second wife, to the deceased first wife:
I will take on your children — out of love for you.

Parents and Children

Father, with terminal illness, to his children:
I am entrusting you to your mother — with love.

Mother, whose husband died early, to her children:
In you I also love and honor your father. He is still here for you, through me.

Divorced mother to her children, seeing that they hate their father:
I loved your father very much, and if you become like him, I assent to that.

Woman who would have preferred to marry another man to her children:
For you, your father is the best.

Mother and father to an aborted child:
My dear child.
I take you now as my child, and you may have me as your mother/your father.
and
I am sorry.
I am now giving you a place in my heart, and you shall have a part of the good that
I shall bring about in memory of you and consideration of you.

Children and Parents

Child to father and mother, bowing to them deeply:
I give to you — both of you — honor.

Son to his mother, who died giving birth to him:
Dear Mother, please bless me.

Son, wanting to follow his father, to his father, who died in prison for his convictions:
I will not let you go unless you bless me.

Son to his father, who became culpable in the war:
Father, I let you go, whatever your fate and your guilt.

Terminally ill son to his father, while still unable to bow before him:
Please, give me a little extra time.

Child to father who has killed himself:
I bow to your decision and to your fate.
You will always remain my father, and I will always remain your child.

Son of an alcoholic father, to his mother:
Mother, I assert to you that I will respect my father, just like you.

Daughter, whom the father identifies with his former wife, to her father as she points to her mother:
She is my mother, and I am her daughter.
She is the only right one for me.
I have nothing to do with that other one.

This same daughter to her mother:
You are my mother, and I am your daughter.
You are the right one for me.
I have nothing to do with Father's new wife.

Son, whom the mother identifies with her former husband, to his mother as he points to his father:
He is my father, and I am his son.
Only he is the right one for me.
I have nothing to do with that other one.

This same son to his father:
You are my father, and I am your son.
You are the right one for me.
I have nothing to do with Mother's new husband.

Son to his mother, when she speaks disparagingly about his father:
In seeing him, you are also seeing me.

Daughter to her mother, when she is afraid of becoming like her:
Look, I have become just like you, and I am content with that.

Siblings

Woman to her older sister, who took care of her as a child:
I know what you gave me. I respect it and it accompanies me.

Woman to her brother, whom she feels might not be a good father to his son:
For him, you are the best.

Man to his older brother, who died early:
I respect you as my big brother,
You are the first, and I am the second.

Child of unmarried parents, to the younger siblings, from whom it had been kept secret:
I am your sister/your brother.

Woman to her older brother, for whose guilt she is atoning:
I respect your fate, and I remain with mine.

Giving and Receiving

Mother to her son, at whose birth she became ill:
I was glad to give you life, even at this price. You may keep
the gift — it will make me happy.

*Child to parents, who married for the child's sake, and who are
unhappy:*
Whatever the blame or the guilt may be between you — I
accept what you gave me with love.

Child to the mother, who was injured in birth process:
Dear Mother, as you paid such a heavy price for my life, it
shall not have been in vain.

Woman to her mother, who died in childbirth:
Mother, dear Mother, this was really terrible.
And, pointing to her family:
Look, life has continued in a good way.
I am passing on what you have given to me.

Child to mother who gave the child up for adoption:
Mother, if it relieves you of a burden, I will carry it willingly.

Adopted child, on seeing the mother again:
I am happy that you gave birth to me.

Remaining

Child to parents, seeing that one of them wants to leave or die:
Dear Father, Dear Mother,
even though you may leave, I will stay.
I will always honor you.
You will always remain my father. You will always remain
my mother.

*Child to someone in the family to whom the child wants to say,
"I would rather die than you:"*
Dear Father (or Mother, or Brother, or Sister), even though
you leave, I will stay.
And:
Dear Father (or Dear Mother), please bless me,
even though you are leaving and I am staying.

*Child to deceased family members, when this child does not dare
to live because they are dead:*
Dear Father (or Mother, or Brother, or Sister), you are dead.
I will live a while longer, then I will die also.
Or:
I will complete what has been given to me, as long as it lasts.
Then I too will die.

*Mother who wanted to die, to her little daughter, who had fallen
deathly ill:*
I will stay — and I will be happy if you also stay.

Woman to her great-grandmother, who had died in childbirth:
Please be friendly, if I stay with my husband and my child.

Anorexic daughter to her father, who wants to leave:
Dear Father, even if you leave — I will stay. I stay with
Mother.

And to her mother:
Mother, even if Father leaves, I will stay.

Anorexic daughter to the deceased siblings of her father, as she sees that he wants to follow them:
Please bless my father if he remains with us, and bless me when I remain with my father.

Bulimic girl, for whom eating means wanting to live and purging means wanting to die, to her father:
Father, I'm staying. I like what I get to eat with you.
I accept it gladly from you.

Compulsive gambler to his grandfather and father, seeing that he wants to follow them into death:
I would rather gamble my money away than my life.

Solving

Father to his son, who holds him in contempt:
Listen, my son: I am your father, and you are my son.

Father, heavily disabled from the war, to his daughter, who wants to take on his suffering:
I will bear it myself. As far as I'm concerned, you are free.

Child to parents who mistreated the child:
It was terrible. Nevertheless, I will make something of my life.

Husband to his wife who was abused as a child:
Allow yourself to love them, then you are free.

When someone has made a mistake, and suffers from it:
I made a mistake, and now I accept the consequences.

Daughter to her mother who told her she was a whore:
Mother, so I am — a little bit.

Woman who wants to object immediately when someone says something unfair:
There is something in that.

Leave-taking and Peace

Child to parents, upon growing up and leaving:
I accept what you have given me.
It was a great deal, and it was enough.
The rest I will do myself.
And now I leave you in peace.

Man and woman to each other, at their separation:
I accept what you have given me. It is a great deal.
I will take it with me and honor it always.
For what went wrong between us, I accept my part of the re-
sponsibility,
and leave you with your part.
And now I leave you in peace.

Parents to their child who died:
We gladly gave you your life and gladly did for you every-
thing that we did.
We let you go now, in peace.
Yet for us you will always remain our child, and we your
parents.

Father to son who killed himself:
I hold for you a place in my heart.
You will always remain my son, and I your father.

Child to father who killed himself:
I respect your fate and your decision.
You should know that things have worked out well.
And now you can have your peace.

Daughter to her father, whom she found dead, having killed himself:
Dear Father, within me you are still alive, and within me you are doing well.
I will let you participate in what I do.

Mother to her son, who died in an accident, and for whom she still grieves:
I respect your life and your death.

Daughter to her father, who died when she was still little:
Dear Father, you are still here within me.

Concluding Comments

Order and Fullness

Order is the form or pattern of disparate phenomena working together.
Therefore, multiplicity and fullness are of its essence.

Order functions through exchange,
drawing together that which is dispersed
and gathering it for consummation.
Therefore, movement is of its essence.

Order attracts transitory phenomena
into a form that promises continuity.
Therefore, duration is of its essence.

Just as a tree, before it falls, releases the fruit that will survive it,
so does order fade away with time.
Therefore, renewal and change are of its essence.

The living patterns of order vibrate and unfold.
They drive us and discipline us,
through longing and fear.
In setting us boundaries, they also give us freedom.

They lie beyond that which separates us.

Concluding Story

Condensation

A learned man asked a wise man
how the particular becomes part of a whole,
and how knowledge of many things is different from knowledge
of fullness.

The wise man answered:
"That which is widely dispersed becomes a whole,
when it finds a center,
and works in a collected manner.
For only through a center does multiplicity
become essential and effective;
and its fullness then appears to us as simplicity,
almost small,
a quiet power moving along to the next thing,
remaining below,
close to that which carries.

"Therefore, in order to experience fullness,
or to communicate it,
I do not need to know all the particulars,
nor to say them, or have them, or do them.

"If you want to enter the town,
you pass through a single gate.
When you ring the bell once,
you cause many other tones to sound as well.
And he who has plucked the ripe apple,
does not need to fathom its origin.
He holds it in his hand and eats it."

The learned man objected that surely in order to know the truth,
one had to know all the details.

The wise man, however, countered by saying:
"Only in regard to the old truths do we know a great deal.
The truths that continue,
are bold and new.
They conceal their outcome, as the seed conceals the tree.
He who hesitates to act,
because he wants to know more than is possible with the next step,
misses the actual.
He takes the coin for the merchandise;
and from the trees he makes wood."

The learned man suggested that that could only be part of the answer,
and requested further explanation.

The wise man however declined,
saying that fullness is at first like a keg full of cider —
sweet and turbid.
It requires time to ferment,
and become clear.
If you then drink it, instead of tasting it,
you begin to stagger.

Many in the field of psychotherapy will recognize BERT HELLINGER's contribution to it as a unique integration of diverse elements. Former priest and missionary to the Zulu, with a wide range of subsequent psychotherapeutic experience, Hellinger has forged an approach that is at once a synthesis of and a departure from familiar healing paradigms. His insistence on seeing what is as opposed to blindly accepting what we're told — combined with an unwavering loyalty to and trust in one's own soul — is the foundation upon which this work has been built.

RALPH METZNER, PH.D. is professor of psychology at the California Institute of Integral Studies in San Francisco, as well as a psychotherapist and workshop leader. Dr. Metzner has published widely, and his books include *The Well of Remembrance*, *The Unfolding Self*, and *Green Psychology*.